Brand Power Builder

How To Defeat Website Hijackers, Rescue Internet Orphans and Win Brand Independence Online

Duncan W. Moss
mossmediasolutions.com

Copyright ©2016 by Duncan W. Moss

ALL RIGHTS ARE RESERVED. No part of this publication may be reproduced or transmitted in any form or by any means, mechanically or electronically, including photocopying and recording or by any information storage or retrieval system without permission in writing from the Publisher.

Published by Amazon.com

DISCLAIMER AND/OR LEGAL NOTICE
To protect the privacy of certain individuals the names and identifying details have been changed. The information contained within this book is strictly for educational purposes. If you wish to apply ideas contained in this book, you are taking full responsibility for your actions. Although the author and publisher have made every effort to ensure that the information in this book was correct at press time, the author and publisher do not assume and hereby disclaim any liability to any party for any loss, damage, or disruption caused by errors or omissions, whether such errors or omissions result from negligence, accident, or any other cause.

Preface

I've written this book to function as a working guide rather than a traditional business book so that you can find the information you need quickly and easily.

To get the most out of this book I suggest you read it the order it's been written because what's offered here is a step-by-step system designed to help you safeguard your brand and avoid big mistakes that could cripple your ability to grow your business or not-for-profit online.

But if you read nothing else, be sure to check out the sections on "The Basics of Building Brand Power" and "Brand Platform".

I wish you every success in your future endeavors and I hope that I am able to help you avoid the common pitfalls so many business owners suffer when attempting to establish their brand online.

Best Regards,

Duncan Moss

Table of Contents

What Is a Brand Anyway? 12
What's in a Name? 15
Tip 1 16
Orphaned Websites 17
Website Hijacking Scenario One: The Ransom 18
Tip 2 18
Website Hijacking Scenario Two: Ripe for the Picking 19
Case Study 1 Man Buys Google.com for $12 20
Case Study 2 The Case of the Forgotten Domain 21
Tip 3 22
Website Hijacking Scenario Three: Proprietary Code 23
Tip 4 25
Case Study 3 The Case of the Missing Project Files 26
Case Study 4 The Case of the Out-of-Control Webmaster 29
Who Holds the Keys to Your Brand Online? 30
Tip 5 30
Case Study 5 The Case of the 'Free' Website 31
Case Study 6 The Case of The Friendly Domain Hijacker 32
Case Study 7 The Offer You Can't Refuse But Should 33
Does Your Dog Bite? Asking The Right Questions 36
The Truth About DIY Web Builders 38
The Benefits of Brand Power Building 39
Why You Need Brand Power 40
Who the Heck Am I and Why Listen to Me? 41

Brand Power Building: The Basics	*42*
Step 1: Research Now and Avoid Regret Later	*47*
Step 2: Secure and Protect Your Brand Credentials	*51*
Tip 6	*54*
Step 3: Choose to be Hosted Not Taken Hostage	*55*
Step 4: Backup Your Website, Backup Your Brand	*56*
Case Study 7 The Mystery of The Abandoned Website	*59*
Step 5: Adopt Brand Management Best Practices	*62*
Step 6: Achieve Online Independence with Content Management Software	*68*
Step 7: Avoid Tyranny, Demand Transparency and Training	*70*
Step 8: Registering Your Business Name, Brand Name, Trade Name and Trademark	*73*
Tip 7	*74*
Step 9: Build and Grow Your Brand Platform	*79*
Take-aways and Closing Thoughts	*86*
Additional Resources	*88*

Introduction
Why Should You Care?

Imagine investing hundreds (more likely thousands) of dollars in developing your website and online brand only to see every penny wasted.

Believe it or not, this happens every day to an uncountable number of businesses large and small. Businesses run by smart and savvy people just like you.

That's why I'm going to show you what to do if you find yourself struggling to solve any one of the top four problems business owners face when they attempt to enter the world of online marketing.

> Before you:
>
> 1. Lose control of your brand online because you own an Orphaned Website;
>
> 2. Become victim to an Online Hijacking and are forced to spend huge sums of money to keep your brand alive online;
>
> 3. Get swept up in media mania and lose your shirt in the online advertising game and or;
>
> 4. Discover that your reputation online is non-existent or poor,
>
>   read on.

I'm also going to show you how to protect and promote your brand online. I know that's a tall order but stay with me. You'll come away with a new perspective regarding brand management and real tools as well as information you can use immediately to enhance and control your brand online.

Nine Steps to Brand Power Online

1. Research Now and Avoid Regret Later

2. Secure and Protect Your Brand Credentials

3. Choose to be Hosted Not Taken Hostage

4. Backup your Website, Backup your Brand

5. Adopt Brand Management Best Practices

6. Employ Content Management Web Design

7. Choose Transparency and Training over Tyranny

8. Register Your Business, Brand Trade Names

9. Build and Grow a Brand Platform

Failure to understand and implement these nine steps to protect yourself and your business online could easily cripple or close your business before it even gets started.

Knowing how to manage and protect your online brand can make the difference between success or failure, online as well as offline.

It's been my experience that business owners as well as many web developers don't understand the importance of online brand management and so they become victims of, or unwitting perpetrators of, preventable online disasters.

But before we go too deeply into how you safely build a brand online I think we need to take a moment to consider what a brand really is.

What Is a Brand Anyway?

To paraphrase Wikipedia, a brand is a name or symbol that distinguishes one seller's product from its competitors.

This may be true but there's more to it than that. From a marketing and public relations standpoint a brand is the personality or reputation of a business, based on how its customers and staff perceive it.

Many people think of brand in terms of the symbol or logo that a company uses but the nature of their experience with a particular business, good or bad, is their real sense of brand. That personal experience is what determines a business's personality or reputation as far as customers are concerned.

As you can imagine, reputation influences brand far more than any logo or slogan ever will. It determines how people feel about your business and whether they will ever consider purchasing your products or services. This is why reputation management is one of the most important aspects of a business's brand.

But in the age of social media, reputation management is not what it used to be. Unlike the early days of advertising you can no longer be the dominant voice in public discourse about your business. Controlling everything that's published or broadcast about your business is now impossible. This is why the development and on-going management of your Brand Platform is so critical to the health of your business.

I've devoted a whole section to Brand Platform at the end of this book but for now I'll offer this simple definition.

A Brand Platform is a marketing system that invites prospects and clients to join in the on-going conversation with you and your team about your products and services. Outbound unidirectional Brand Platform tools include, but are not limited to, books, display advertising and video. Inbound bi-directional tools include website blogs, social media, live events and word of mouth to name a few.

The connection between reputation and platform must be understood if you actually want to build a brand online. Many business owners ignore, or are unaware of, just how critical a platform is to their business.

Because everything from social media posts, traditional advertising, newsletters, email and one to one communication with clients are all part of your Brand Platform you need a strategic plan in order to manage it all. Although this may sound complicated it doesn't have to be.

Simply deciding that you will use Facebook and not Twitter is a strategic decision about your Brand Platform. Choosing to publish a monthly newsletter that is of real interest to your clients is also a Brand Platform strategy. All of these things contribute to the overall impression you leave with others about your business.

Managing and growing your business's Brand Platform is of course, a big part of what we all know as marketing. And as I expect you know, there is more to marketing than slapping together a few flyers or posting the odd thing on Facebook.

I'll come back to the subject of reputation management and Brand Platform later, when we examine this concept in detail but right now we need to start with something more basic: the selection and protection of the name of your business in all its different forms.

What's in a Name?

I want ask you a question. How many business owners can tell you where their website domain is registered or where it's hosted?

And how many business owners know the passwords or the renewal dates for their website?

In my experience the answer is too few.

Imagine not bothering to commit your business address to memory and the trouble you'd have if you didn't know exactly where your office was.

Imagine trusting a stranger with all your important business information and the havoc that could ensue as a result. When it comes to online branding, these are the kinds of scenarios many business owners find themselves in.

Consider the fact that thousands of new domains are registered every day and that more and more businesses now depend on their website for economic success. What's really surprising about this exponential online growth is just how often and how easily websites become orphaned or hijacked.

These are two very preventable scenarios that can spell serious trouble for unsuspecting business owners if precautions aren't taken to avoid them.

All too often, I meet business owners who want their website re-designed but don't have the passwords or critical information needed to access their site. Even worse, I've met business owners who have lost control of their brand online, thanks to a simple oversight or because of the unscrupulous actions of others.

Imagine not knowing where you left the keys to your business or worse yet finding out that someone else is using your business name!

Additionally, I speak with webmasters who have not taken the time to ensure the 'keys' to their clients' website are actually in their clients' hands. Things as critical as website access codes must be safely stored and managed so that both the client and the webmaster can manage the brand easily, efficiently and securely.

> **Tip 1**
> Be sure to collect all the documentation, project files and complete downloadable backups of your website. Then store them in a safe place, separate from your website hosting server.

Orphaned Websites

It's not uncommon to have had a friend, family member or small company build your website when you first launched your business. It was free or cheap which was great at the time but now you need something more. Unfortunately your wanna-be webmaster doesn't do websites anymore because he or she moved on to other things. You're not sure where the domain was registered or where your site is hosted and worse still you don't have the passwords. And the last straw is that the only person who did have all this information hasn't returned your calls or emails. Your website is now an orphan.

You may have had the resources to hire a local web designer to build your site. It looked good... five years ago. But you haven't made changes to it in ages and now you realize it's time for an update and you want your website to really start working for you. Unfortunately your old web designer has moved on.

Or worse still, he or she doesn't have your project files anymore. And since you didn't use a content management system like WordPress there's no easy way to update the site. Your website has just become an orphan.

The good news is, this situation can be fixed with a little know-how and time. But properly armed with the right information, you could have prevented this from happening entirely and saved yourself a lot of frustration and cash.

Website Hijacking Scenario One: The Ransom

Who knew that someone might be gunning for your brand online? Imagine you're ready to purchase a domain name that matches the name of your new business only to discover someone else owns it and they want a king's ransom to sell it. Your brand has been hijacked even before you get out of the gate!

You could consider using a .biz, .net or .org domain extension to get the name you want but if someone already owns the .com URL you're going to lose traffic to them because the majority of online users just assume .com is the normal URL extension.

> **Tip 2**
> Research your domain name availability before you commit money, time and resources to a brand name.

Website Hijacking Scenario Two: Ripe for the Picking

Imagine that you've spent months, possibly years promoting your brand online. Add to that, you've spent big money on your website in an effort to attract new customers.

Then one morning you discover your website is gone. Why?

Because you didn't buy domain protection. In fact, you didn't even know it existed. Now, because you forgot to renew your domain name, your competitor snatched it up and all your hard work is gone for good. Your website's been hijacked.

Case Study 1
Man Buys Google.com for $12

Ex-Google employee, Sanmay Ved was the lucky buyer of "Google.com," if only for a minute or two.

Ved said, "*I used to work at Google so I keep messing around with the product. I typed in Google.com and to my surprise it showed it as available. I thought it was some error, but I could actually complete the checkout.*"

Sanmay Ved added it to his shopping cart and, surprisingly, the transaction went through.

To get the full story visit this link.

http://www.businessinsider.com/this-guy-bought-googlecom-from-google-for-one-minute-2015-9

This may sound like an unlikely scenario but if it can happen to Google it can happen to you. Buy domain protection.

Case Study 2
The Case of the Forgotten Domain

The owner of a local transportation firm in my area, let's call them *Terry's Trucking*, had assigned the management of the company website to his business manager. But when the business manager moved on to a new job with another company he didn't give the TerrysTrucking.com website another thought and frankly neither did Terry, the owner of the company.

The owner hired a new manager who quickly got to work learning the day to day operations of the business and was too busy to give the website any serious thought.

As it happened, it was about this same time that the domain registration for the website was due for renewal.

No one at Terry's Trucking took notice; not the owner, who didn't normally deal with such things, and certainly not the new business manager, who was focused on learning the ropes of a very busy operation.

No one in the company noticed the day their domain name or their online brand expired. Unfortunately for them, their competition was on the ball and snatched up the expired domain name and still uses it to this day to re-direct traffic to their own website. This is a business that's well known in my area and has had the same name for decades, not to mention the same domain name for well over 10 years.

If they had had their domain registration set to auto-renew, Terry's Trucking wouldn't be losing customers to their competition. But day after day, people search online for Terry's Trucking, click on the web link and find themselves on the home page of his competitor. It's a very hard lesson in domain protection.

Tip 3

Set-up **auto-renew** on your domain name and hosting package. Purchase **domain protection** as well and prevent your brand from being hijacked. Most domain registrars will give you a 30 day grace period, which is handy if for some reason your credit card expires and your domain ends up in Internet limbo.

Website Hijacking Scenario Three: Proprietary Code

You spent good money to develop a great looking website but every time you want to make a change it costs a small fortune. The software that was used to develop your site is either proprietary, complicated or expensive, and you don't know how to make simple changes on your own. Again you've been hijacked!

I'm aware of several situations where large organizations paid for custom-designed, custom-built websites that only the designers know how to run.

In this scenario the designer/developer can charge whatever they feel like for the simplest of changes. And I can tell you, I've been witness to situations that are tantamount to highway robbery when it comes to this sort of thing.

In this day and age there is really no reason for custom coded websites. Yes it's true, you many need the occasional special function or want a feature custom coded but it's important to know that there are many fabulous off-the-shelf web building tools like WordPress, Drupal and Joomla! that can make a website do everything except make coffee.

Over the last few years a number of very sophisticated, easy-to-use web design tools have emerged that allow business owners to build beautiful, highly-interactive websites without having to know anything about coding or even design for that matter.

These website design tools are called Content Management Systems or CMS for short.

> **Content Management System Definition:**
>
> A **Content Management System** (CMS) is computer software that allows you to create and modify your website content using a simple menu that puts an end to the need for almost all coding or programming and it supports multiple users working in a collaborative environment.

Content Managements Systems like WordPress have revolutionized website development. And in my opinion, WordPress should be your first port of call when it comes to web design software. It's now the world's most popular web development software and for good reason. It's open source (nobody owns it), it's easy to use and continues to get better with every passing month. That's because it's supported by the world's largest community of open minded and generous web developers.

Content Management Software Options

Free and Open Source
- WordPress
- Drupal
- Joomla!
- DotNetNuke
- Magneto

Gated (Not Free and Not Open Source)
- Weebly
- SquareSpace

> **Tip 4**
> Use Content Management System (CMS) software and avoid custom coded websites. Custom coded websites only benefit web developers not business owners.

Here's a great source for details and comparisons.

http://www.toptenreviews.com/business/internet/best-content-management-system-software/

Case Study 3
The Case of the Missing Project Files

I was chatting with the owner of a local restaurant one evening. We're friendly enough and run businesses in the same neighborhood, so he has a sense of the nature of my work.

He was bemoaning the fact that while he was pleased with the look of his website, some of the information is no longer valid -- his menu needs updating and his hours of operation need to be changed as the seasons change. His problem is that he can't track down the web designer who has the original project files for his website.

Because his website was not based on a Content Management System (CMS) like WordPress his website and his brand are now floating out there in cyberspace - invalid, unattended, and, worse yet, inaccessible. In other words, it's orphaned.

When it comes to project based software like Dreamweaver or CoffeeCup, the website project lives on the developer's hard drive and must be uploaded to the hosting server before changes can be made live.

Before WordPress and other CMS software came along this was how almost all websites were developed. It's for this reason that I made it standard practice in my business to upload my client's website project files to the server where the website is hosted. That way my clients have access to everything needed to manage their website. If I were to win the lottery and disappear to a beautiful tropic island, my clients would have everything they need so that another web developer could take over from where I left off.

I started asking other people - friends and business associates - if they have access to their website's project files and more often than not, I would get blank stares. They simply didn't know. Before it's too late and while you know how to contact your web designer, ask them this question.

"Are all of my project files, including the design files, metadata and website backups on the server with my website?" You should also ask for a copy of all this data to be sent to you on a USB stick for safekeeping.

In doing so you ensure that no matter what changes you make in your business, or in your relationship with your webmaster or designer, you'll have the blueprints and all the working files for your website.

It's frustrating enough to know your site is not current, and that you're helpless to change it. It's another thing again to be faced with the cost of a complete rebuild because you don't have the project files or metadata for your site.

Using a CMS like WordPress or Drupal is, in my estimation, the best way to prevent your website from becoming orphaned. It's for this reason, no doubt, that the vast majority of websites online today are CMS based.

> *Your website is the hub of your online brand.*
> *If you allow it to become an orphaned asset*
> *or hijacked, you put your brand and your*
> *business in serious jeopardy.*

Case Study 4
The Case of the Out-of-Control Webmaster

Before I had officially entered the web design and development business I was producing videos and also offered video encoding for the web. A client of mine asked if I could encode the new video I had produced for him so that his webmaster could post it on his web site. I said "sure, that's easy; I just need to know what video format and size your web master would prefer".

The answer never came, even after repeated requests. It appeared that this particular webmaster either didn't know how to post a video online or just didn't care about his client. In the end I developed a new WordPress website for this client because the original webmaster refused to give his client control his own website.

I've run across possessive and out of control webmasters on more than one occasion. It appears to be a relatively common phenomenon which can present a very serious problem for business owners. In my opinion if you paid for it, it's yours. And if you choose to engage a new web designer you have every right to do so.

It's my belief that the more a business owner knows about his or her website and online brand, the more he or she will be able to attract the right kind of new customers and grow their business.

Who Holds the Keys to Your Brand Online?

The best way to ensure that your webmaster can't get complete control of your website is to ensure that the domain registration is in your name and that you are the only one who knows the password to your domain registrar account. In addition to this, be sure you have an up-to-date, off-site backup of your website.

Any self-respecting webmaster will understand why you will want to have your domain registered in your name as well as an off-site backup of the website. In turn, they will most likely ask that you not tinker with the structure of your website or the database, which is a fair request. Just like any complex technology, it's best to leave certain things to the experts, but that doesn't mean you give them unrestricted access and control of your most valuable online asset either.

> **Tip 5**
> Make it extremely clear from the outset that your webmaster is a guest in your website, not the owner.

Case Study 5
The Case of the 'Free' Website

Another client of mine asked me one day just how much it would cost to upload a video to their website and update some the text on the page. Again, I wasn't the developer of the site, but I said that uploading a 5-minute video doesn't take very long and if they knew what the text changes were the whole job shouldn't take more than an hour or two at the most. To my surprise (to my horror really) I discovered that they had paid almost $5,000 to have this work done. Since the client in question knew nothing about web development or management they were at the mercy of their webmaster. That's what I call website hijacking, plain and simple.

The back story here is that the web developer offered to build the website for next to nothing, which they did. A year later, when this custom coded site needed updates the client was at the mercy of this devious developer. If it sounds too good to be true, it probably is.

If they had chosen a CMS, the client could have done this work themselves but because of the website's custom code, they were at the mercy of the developer.

Case Study 6
The Case of The Friendly Domain Hijacker

Eating lunch one day, I overheard a restaurant owner complaining to her friend that she was stuck with a very expensive monthly bill for her website. A local online directory that offered information on where to dine in our city had learned she was about to open a new restaurant, quickly registered the domain name of her restaurant (before she did) and then offered to promote it through the directory for "just $500 a month." They had hijacked her domain name and were holding it ransom. For $500 a month! And all they were offering was a listing in their directory. I suggested she call her lawyer and have the firm send a letter offering $50 for the domain or legal action would be taken. She was lucky. They sold the domain back to her for that price.

In reality the dining directory had no obligation to sell the domain back to the restaurateur. It wasn't a very nice thing to do but they legally owned the domain name for her restaurant.

This kind of thing has happened to celebrities and small business owners alike. It's domain name hijacking, as far as I'm concerned, and I'm surprised it's not illegal.

Case Study 7
The Offer You Can't Refuse But Should

A couple of years ago, a large Canadian bank teamed up with a very well-known search engine and a web hosting service. They did this in an effort to help more businesses get online. At that time less than 50% of local businesses in North America had a website, which I'm sure you know has changed significantly over the last few years. Now more than 80% of all businesses in North America have a website.

The web hosting service offered a year of free hosting and access to an easy to use, do-it-yourself web design tool. On the surface it sounded like a great deal. And when a major bank teams up with a world-renowned search engine to suggest you take the free one-year deal, you'd think it would be an offer you could trust. But as I've already stated, "if it seems too good to be true, it probably is."

I decided to investigate and here's what I discovered. The web hosting company did indeed offer a year of free hosting and free domain registration. And the do-it-yourself web design tool was easy to use but the templates were definitely dated and didn't offer any real originality in design. In other words your website wasn't going to be distinctive but what do you expect for free?

What I found most disturbing was the degree to which the web hosting company constantly tried to up-sell new users to purchase overpriced add-ons to improve their free websites. I could see why they would try, since the introductory offer was on their dime, but the cost of the add-ons just didn't add up to real value, in my opinion.

Looking a little deeper, my biggest fear was realized. The entire scheme was a well-crafted online hijacking. Hard to believe when you consider who was putting their seal of approval on everything.

Here's what unsuspecting users wouldn't discover until it was too late. If they took the free, one-year hosting deal and spent the time to build their online business brand using the free web building software service, they would never be able to move the site! The web hosting provider didn't offer users a way to backup or export the contents of their website so they would never be able to leave without leaving all their content behind and losing all the time they had invested. Just like the line from the Eagle song, "you can check out any time you like but you can never leave."

This free website hosting deal was akin to getting an apartment where you move in with your furniture and personal belongings but when you outgrow the place there is no way to get your stuff out. Users of this scheme were in fact hijacked.

Imagine spending hours of your precious time uploading pictures and original content, working on layout and the color scheme, and making the free hosting service a cozy home for your website and online business. A year or so later, you realize that you've outgrown the cookie cutter look and it's limited features. You want a more customized site - something with more specialized features, but you discover there's no way to backup or export all that you've created and take it with you. You're stuck with what the hosting provider has to offer or you move on, leaving everything behind and forced to start from scratch.

I was appalled to discover that a major Canadian bank and leading search engine would support such a scheme but they did. I'll give them the benefit of the doubt and suggest that they didn't look closely at the hosting provider's offering or, in fact, didn't know what to look for.

This story is just one many that has inspired me to write this book and to create the ***Brand Power Builder System.***

> **If you're interested in seeing exactly how the Brand Power Builder System works and the tools you can use to achieve brand independence online visit BrandPowerBuilder.com to watch the training video.**

Does Your Dog Bite?
Asking The Right Questions

I believe everyone has a right to know what they're getting into when it comes to establishing their brand online, especially when it means investing lots of time and money.

The trick is to know what questions to ask. I'm reminded of a scene from an old Pink Panther film, "The Pink Panther Strikes Again", 1976. In it, Inspector Clouseau visits an Alpine inn managed by a strange old innkeeper. The minute Clouseau enters the inn, he is confronted by a snarling dog. Concerned, Clouseau asks the innkeeper, "Does your dog bite?" The innkeeper replies, "No." A moment later the dog bites Clouseau. Shaking the dog off his leg, Clouseau says, "I thought you said your dog doesn't bite!" The innkeeper replies, "That's not my dog."

Here is a link to the scene on YouTube.
http://www.youtube.com/watch?v=jcXEtKSRI8Y
As you can see, he didn't ask the right question and, as a result, got bitten. When it comes to establishing your brand online, this is one of the biggest pitfalls - not knowing which questions to ask.

Here is a list of questions every business owner should ask before handing over hard earned cash and their brand to a web developer or designer.

Questions to Ask Contract Web Developers

- Are you using an open source, content management system to build my site?
- Will you give me a copy of all the source files used to create my website?
- Will you make sure that my domain and web hosting account are registered in my name?
- Will you set me up as an Administrator of my website so that I have full access to and complete control of my website?
- Will you provide training so that I, or my staff, can make changes to the site ourselves?
- Do you offer a guarantee that my website will function without error and get backed up regularly?
- Do you offer on-going maintenance and how much will it cost?

The Truth About DIY Web Builders

If you're considering a DIY style web design service, find out if they offer a data and media export option. If not, look elsewhere.

Weebly is a great example of a DIY web design service that lets you export all your content so that if you decide sometime later you need a more robust site, you simply hit the export button to download all your content and away you go.

Odds are, you'll move your content more than once before you settle in with a web hosting provider and a web design that suits you, so be sure you can export all your content and that you can create regular backups of your site.

If you become the unwitting victim of either of these two rampant problems, all the hard earned money you've spent on your beautiful website and online branding efforts can be lost overnight.

Now, I'd like to walk you through nine simple steps you should employ to build a secure brand online. They are the foundation on which you can safely build a powerful brand and marketing system.

The Benefits of Brand Power Building

Over the course of the next few pages, you'll learn how to put an end to what I believe are two of the biggest online traps for business owners today.

You'll learn the nine simple steps every successful business owner must take to safely and confidently build a brand online.

You'll never have to spend another nickel to make simple changes or updates to your website ever again.

You'll learn how to control and manage your brand online.

You'll know how to protect your online brand and your investment from scammers and interlopers.

You'll have a clear, easy-to-follow, reproducible blueprint you can use to protect your brand and that you can apply to any new product or service you develop.

You'll be able to strengthen and grow your online brand - confident that you're building on a strong foundation.

Why You Need Brand Power

If Any of the Following Statements Apply to You Then You Really Should Consider Rebuilding Your Brand Online.

1. You own a business and are frustrated with your current webmaster, web developer or designer.

2. You feel you've lost control of your website.

3. You are unable to make simple updates or changes to your website without having to contact your webmaster.

4. You are dissatisfied with your current website design or function.

5. You are about to start a new business.

6. You own a website that isn't working for you and that isn't converting visitors into customers.

7. You have not, or are not getting a return on your internet marketing investment.

Who the Heck Am I and Why Listen to Me?

I've been in the marketing and communications business for over 35 years. Fourteen years ago I started my own company, Moss Media Solutions. At that time, internet marketing was still in its infancy. I built my own website to advertise the business and before I knew it, I was being asked to build websites for other local businesses as well.

I soon discovered that a number of my new website clients were coming to me because they were dealing with either an orphaned website or because they had become victims of a website hijacking.

Since both of these problems can be easily avoided or fixed, I decided it was time to share what I know. Business owners, large and small, need to be able to leverage the investments they make in their websites and safely grow their online brand without fear of losing their investment or losing control of their brand online.

I enjoy helping others develop their brand and grow their business. It's fun and rewarding. What I find frustrating is that many business owners have spent good money after bad on websites and branding efforts that have done nothing for them. I think most people would agree that a website you can't control, or that does nothing to help promote your brand, is just a waste of time and money. After meeting so many entrepreneurs who have lost control over their website, I decided it was time to do something about it.

Brand Power Building: The Basics

1. Research Now and Avoid Regret

All you need to get started are these three free tools:
- The Google Adwords Keyword Planner
- Google's Search Tool and
- GoDaddy's Domain Search Tool

You'll need a Gmail account to access Google's Adwords Keyword Planner but that's all.

Take 20 minutes to research your brand name online and see just how unique it really is. Use these free tools to see if the domain name that matches your business is available. If not, it's time to rethink the game plan or prepare to pay whatever it takes to buy your name back.

2. Secure and Protect Your Brand Credentials

Once you're certain your brand name is relatively unique and you have secured the .com as well as the .ca domain of your business names (or your country code extension), you need to make sure it won't get lost or stolen. Take the time to print out the name of your domain registrar along with the username and password. Now, put it with your mortgage or other important papers.

3. Choose to be Hosted Not Taken Hostage

Where and how you choose to host your website can mean the difference between suffering from hacker hell or enjoying the serenity that comes with security. In short, when it comes to hosting go big or stay home. In other words, choose a large reputable hosting company. This is not the time to get cheap trying to save $20 a year! I recommend GoDaddy. I'll explain why in the detailed breakdown on hosting.

4. Backup Your Website Backup Your Brand

No matter where you host your website, be sure to arrange for weekly backups that you can download. It's cheap and easy to set up, no matter what kind of site you have. This is a set-it and forget-it task that could save you thousands of dollars. I'll provide more in-depth information on this process in the detailed section on Website Backups.

5. Adopt Brand Best Practices

Establishing and employing Brand Best Practices doesn't have to be an arduous task but it does take careful thought.

One of the best ways to get started is to have a look at what truly successful brands are doing and don't limit your research to just your market niche. Some of the most innovative ideas have come as a result of recognizing best practices in one industry and then adapting them to work in a completely different business sector.
Here are the top four best practices that are, in my opinion, consistent with the most successful brands.

- Be Customer Focused
- Be Unique
- Be Values-Driven, Have a Mission and Vision
- Be Proactive – Make Offers

6. Employ Content Management Software CMS to Achieve Online Independence

Use content management software, like WordPress, Joomla! or Drupal to have your site built. I'd suggest WordPress and I'm not alone there. It's now the world's most popular web development system for a reason. Yes it's true, there are more robust and flexible CMS options than WordPress but none of them are as easy to use as WordPress. You'll find more information on this topic in detailed section on Content Management Systems.

7. Avoid Tyranny, Demand Transparency Training

No matter who you choose to help you develop your online brand and website, be sure they document everything they do and send you copies of those documents. You'll want domain and hosting company names, usernames and passwords as well as expiration dates. Nothing less. You should also get a step-by-step walkthrough of how and where to access your website.

8. Register Your Business, Brand, Trade Name and Trademark

This is a big topic that goes beyond the scope of this book but here's the short version. Registering your business name and trade names with your local Joint Stock Registry is an absolute necessity, even if you're just a one-man band. Registering nationally is necessary if you plan to set up offices or a franchise outside your local jurisdiction. Registering a Trade Name takes time and money but should be given serious consideration if you want protection for your brand on a national level.

9. Build and Grow a Brand Platform

Without a platform, your business really doesn't have a brand. That's because your brand is really the reputation of your business. Contrary to popular belief your brand is not your logo. Choosing how and where people learn about your business is how you build your platform and, in turn, your brand.

Social media for example is a part of your brand platform, so is your customer service style, your newsletter, your website and Facebook page as well as your advertising, not to mention what others say about your business. Without a clear plan to grow and manage your platform, your brand will grow uncontrolled and will become determined more by what others say than what you want it to be.

Brand Power Building Strategies: Detailed

Step 1: Research Now and Avoid Regret Later

Research is one of those tasks that is often overlooked or avoided when it comes to building a website or launching a brand online, but it's critical to success.

You might be asking, why do I need to do brand name research? Well, let's assume for a moment you're about to open an auto body shop and your name is Bob. So you figure Bob's Auto Body is a great name for your business.

If you search Google you'll discovery that someone in Boston already owns BobsAutobody.com. Imagine if you had already paid a lawyer to legally register your business name or paid a graphic designer to create a unique logo for your business?

It's true that you might be able to secure the .net or .org version of the name but most people will search for the .com version of your business name if they're looking for you online. In Canada you could get away with using the .ca but that's still less than ideal.

If you really want to build a strong brand online you need a unique brand name for which the .com and .ca (or your country code) are available. You should purchase both the .com and your country code extension to ensure no one else can have them.

Now let's take a look your market or niche. We're going to use the Google Adwords Keyword Planner for this. In order to use this free tool, you'll need a Gmail account which is free.

After logging into your Gmail account, enter the following URL in your browser address bar:

https://www.google.ca/adwords/get-started/

and follow the instructions.

Don't worry. You won't be expected to spend any money or set up an ad campaign if you don't want to.

Once you're inside your new Google Adwords Account select "Tools" from the top menu and "Keyword Planner" from the drop down menu.

Now select "Search for New Keywords or Phrases".

In the case of Bob's Auto Body we'd use Google's keyword planner to:

- first select the product which is auto body,
- then the domain name we're planning to use,
- the product category, which in this case Google will suggest is "Collision and Auto body Repair".
- Now we specify the city we're in,
- the language we choose to use (such as English).
- Then click the "Get Ideas" Button.

On the results page, click the "Keyword Ideas" tab and you'll see that Google has extracted a list of keywords that people have actually used to searched for auto body repair services. In this case the top search term is "Auto Body Shop". Now it's time to put GoDaddy's domain search tool to use.

I searched for BobsAutobodyshop.com and discovered that the domain was available. (It may not be available now but it was when I wrote this chapter.) So rather than branding the business **Bob's Autobody** it would be much better to brand it **Bob's Auto Body Shop.** At least that way a unique .com and .ca domain can be purchased and secured without worry. Better still this particular domain name contains the most popular search term on Google for the Collision and Autobody repair niche.

If after doing your research you discover someone else already owns the .com version of your trade name, brand or product, it's time to rethink your plan or prepare to pay whatever it takes to buy your name back.

As you can imagine it's getting harder and harder to secure a unique domain name but here are a few ideas that might help.

Check out GoDaddy's domain auction. The brand name you're hoping for might very well be up for sale. And even if it isn't you might find something better in the auction.

Use GoDaddy's domain search tool to quickly get alternative domain names that are unique and not yet claimed. If you find something you like, you can then apply for a business Trade Name at your local Joint Stock Companies registry. Assuming it's approved, you can then operate your company using a Trade Name that has a unique domain name with a .com extension. This may seem like a lot of trouble but I can assure you it will avoid a great deal of trouble later when you are competing online for the attention of prospective customers.

Use GoDaddy's domain buying service. They'll do their best to negotiate the best price for you and their fees are very reasonable.

Here's a link to a more detailed explanation about the service.

https://ca.godaddy.com/help/what-is-domain-buy-service-1699

Securing a unique .com and .ca domain name for your brand online does take some time, but the alternative is a nightmare. Without it your prospective customers won't find you easily online. And, if they can't find you they won't buy from you.

Just as troublesome is the confusion created by other companies operating online with what appears to be your brand name. You have no control over what they say or how your prospective customers will respond to the mixed signals a situation like this creates.

So, do your research and secure a unique .com domain name that clearly represents your brand. From there you can build a strong foundation for your business online without confusion or clutter from competing brand names.

Step 2:
Secure and Protect Your Brand Credentials

Domain Registrars

So now that you know how to ensure your brand name is a viable domain name that you can use to build your business online, let's look at what's really involved in purchasing and protecting your domain name.

Once you've decided on a domain name that you know for certain will not be confused with anyone else's, it's time to register it.

There are lots of places where you can register a domain name, but my preference is GoDaddy. There are several reasons why I would suggest using GoDaddy for both domain registration as well as hosting.

First is the amazing technical support you'll receive. The second reason I prefer GoDaddy is the tremendous number of options they offer to help you protect your domain name as well as keep it secure and private. And finally, GoDaddy is the world's largest domain registrar and website hosting company.

It's true, there are lots of smaller, very trustworthy registrars out there, but very few of them offer free, 24/7 phone support with wait times under 5 minutes.

To be fully transparent regarding this recommendation, I own and operate MossMediaWebHosting.com which is my GoDaddy reseller portal.

We offer domain registration and hosting services, essentially at cost, as a service to our web design and internet marketing clients. In doing so we are able to guarantee the best technical support in the business because we have GoDaddy as our supplier.

If I won the lottery tomorrow, folded up my tent and decided to spend the rest of my days living the high life, my customers would still receive the best possible service. That's because all the accounts registered through MossMediaWebHosting.com will always be taken care of by GoDaddy whether my company continues to operate or not. This isn't true for many smaller domain registrars who offer similar services.

Now back to the business of actually registering your domain. If you browse on over to GoDaddy.com or MossMediaWebHosting.com and type in your proposed domain name, GoDaddy will tell you if the domain name is available as either a .com, .ca, .net, etc.

If your preferred domain name is available, grab it while you can. You'd be surprised how quickly a good name can get snapped up.

You may notice that the domain you're hoping for is a premium name and, as a result, may cost thousands of dollars to acquire.

As an example if you search for WeightLossforLife you'll see that the .com is available but the cost is over $14,000.

The nice thing about the GoDaddy domain search tool is that it offers alternative domain names. But no matter what's available be certain to secure a .com <u>and</u> .ca version (or your country code). It may be tempting to grab a vanity domain name like WeightLossforLife.tips or WeightLossforLife.club but don't do it if you can't get the .com.

When people search online they assume a .com extension and since getting found online is tough enough, don't make it any harder by counting on people to remember or guess at a vanity extension.

You'll be much better off if you select a relevant .com domain like WeightLossinNewMexico.com or WeightLossinToronto.com than use an obscure domain extension like .buzz or .solutions. If you can't find anything close to a company name and want to describe what you do, but still face problems finding something appropriate, consider adding words or phrases like "info", "today", "foryou", "now", etc.

Assuming you find a suitable .com domain name the next thing to think about is preventing brand confusion online.

So, if you really want to nail down your brand name it's a good idea to purchase the .ca, .org, .net and .info as well.

It usually costs less than $15 annually to register a domain and so for less than $75 you can secure the .com .ca .net .org and .info domains of your brand.
If you take the time and effort to do this, you can be certain there will be no confusing online about who owns your brand.

Before we move on to the next important step in Brand Power Building, there a few more things you should know about registering a domain name.

Once you're certain your brand and domain name are relatively unique and you have secured the .com and .ca domains names of your business you need to make sure it won't get lost or stolen.

I strongly suggest you consider purchasing domain protection so that it can't expire or be transferred without your knowledge or permission.

I've learned to put the expiration date for my domains in my calendar at least a couple of weeks in advance of their expiration date just to be sure the renewal takes place without a hitch.

Something worth considering is making a long-term domain name purchase. This has several advantages.

Google treats domains with a longer registration period with more favor. A five year domain registration won't guarantee a page one position but it can certainly help your page rank.

Longer domain registration periods will also save you money because most hosting providers offer discounts for long term registration.

Tip 6

Don't underestimate the importance or printing out the names of your domain registrar and hosting provider along with the account username and password. Tuck these printouts in a safe place because they are without question the 'keys' to your online kingdom. Also worth knowing and printing is the username and password for you website database. Again ask your webmaster for these.

Step 3:
Choose to be Hosted Not Taken Hostage

Not all hosting companies are made equal and price should not be the only factor in choosing hosting.

As I mentioned earlier, when I outlined the basics step, where and how you choose to host your website can mean the difference between suffering from hacker hell or enjoying the serenity that comes with security. In short when it comes to hosting go big or stay home. In other words choose a large reputable hosting company. Please don't jeopardize your online brand security just to save $20 a year! Once again I'd recommend GoDaddy because they make the whole business of domain purchase, renewal and protect very easy.

Why

The other reason why I believe GoDaddy is a great choice is their tech support. It really is top drawer. Additionally, if you're concerned about hackers GoDaddy offers several solutions to ensure your site is well protected. If your business or organization is involved in politics or controversial issues, hacking can be a real concern, but a top drawer hosting company can help prevent a hacking catastrophe.

Step 4:
Backup Your Website, Backup Your Brand

No matter where you host your website, be sure to arrange for weekly backups that you can download. It's cheap and easy to set up, no matter what kind of site you have. This is a set-it and forget-it task that could save you thousands of dollars.

Again GoDaddy offers website backups as part of their regular hosting service. A call to their tech support toll free number is all it takes to get your site restored. But their backups only go back 30 days. If you want a more extensive backup option you might want to consider purchasing the Backup Buddy plugin for Wordpress. It allows you to make and download your own backups and restore or clone your site anytime, anywhere.

The importance of an off-site or downloadable backup may not be immediately obvious, but without one you will find it almost impossible to change hosting providers or recover from the insertion of malicious content such as malvertising.

It generally pays to have at least two backups of your website created a week apart, and a third one that's 30 days old. The reason for this is that backup files can occasionally be corrupt and/or contain the malware that caused your site to crash. Needless to say, you want this process automated so that you don't have to trouble yourself with such a repetitive task. Like insurance, you hope you never need to use your backup files but you'll be very glad you have them when trouble strikes.

Much like hard drive crashes, it's not a question of *if* your website will crash or become corrupt for some reason, it's just a matter of *when*. Investing time and money in a website that isn't backed up regularly is akin to walking a tightrope without a net.

Here are few WordPress backup software options to consider:

> BackupBuddy
> Backdraft
> Site Vault
> Rackspace
> VaultPress
> BackWPup

Another option is to use a hosting provider that offers a staging area. This feature allows you to make a working copy of your website inside your hosting control panel. The benefit is that you can test changes you'd like to make to your site (especially ones that might break the site) without making them on your live site.

Assuming your changes don't affect the integrity of your site, you can simply override your live site with the new staging area version and now the staged version is your backup. This kind of service does come at a price but if you're making changes to your website on a regular basis, a staging area can be a Godsend.

The hosting company WPEngine offers this feature for WordPress websites. Aquia.com offers this same service for Drupal sites. Before you take this kind of leap in website hosting and make a purchase, check with your webmaster.

A last word on backups. Your website is the heart of your brand online. If you don't have a backup system in place it's only a matter of time before trouble strikes.

You wouldn't drive a car without insurance and for the same reasons you shouldn't invest in a website without a backup system in place.

Case Study 7
The Mystery of The Abandoned Website

To better understand the importance of building a *Power Brand* online I want to share a true story that you may find a little scary.

It all started with a phone call from a friend with a request to help with an orphaned website. In this particular case, the previous webmaster had abandoned the website and his client for reasons that remain unclear to this day.

I agreed to take on the assignment and, after doing a little homework, I uncovered several fairly serious problems. I should mention right now that the website in question was very large, with hundreds of pages. It had tens of thousands of visitors each month and a page-one status on Google in a major and popular niche.

The number of problems with the website were too many to list here but one of the most glaring was that it hadn't been backed up in months. Worse still, the backup was outrageously large and so was the website. Therein lay the first clue in the mystery of the abandoned website. After nearly seven years of use the website had become bloated with huge pictures uploaded by subscribers and staff to the point that it was now 70 gigabytes in size. To put this in perspective, a large website is usually no more than one gigabyte in size. This website was 70 times larger than anything I had ever seen.

The result was a web server so full, it prevented the backup software from running.

But that wasn't the worst of it. Everyone who had access to this website had full administrative rights. Now this might not seem like such a big problem but it proved to be absolutely disastrous. My developer and I had only just begun to outline the scope of work required to whip this website into shape when I received a panicked phone call from the company president. Their website was gone. I was on the road at the time and had to pull over to use my phone to see for myself. Sure enough, no matter how I searched, it was nowhere to be found.

In no time at all, Google started de-indexing many of their pages because they simply didn't exist anymore. Their online presence shrank as the search engines discovered the website was gone. Worse still, ad revenue dropped to zero and subscribers started looking elsewhere for similar content.

To make a long story short, a junior staffer, with complete administrative access to the web server had accidentally deleted the database. To make things worse, the only backup that existed turned out to be corrupt. The website could not be restored.

Seven years of blog posts and photos, not to mention a subscriber list almost a million strong, had been erased with the push of button.

The good news was that we had managed to download a complete copy of this enormous website to our own server along with the subscriber list so all the really important data wasn't lost forever. It took weeks to reconstruct the website is such a way that it was secure, with automated backups and limited user access so that no one could accidentally erase it ever again.

The real reason the previous webmaster abandoned this website may never be known, but my guess is that it became unmanageable and s/he didn't know how to rein it in. The problem was that the inmates were running the asylum. Users were allowed to upload ridiculously huge photos straight from their phones without size restrictions and staffers had complete access to places on the web server that only an experienced and qualified webmaster should have access to.

Protecting your website from accidental damage, as well as malicious attacks, can mean the difference between having a prosperous business and going broke overnight.

The lesson here is that websites, just like cars or homes, must be maintained and kept secure. They require periodic tuneups and backups if they're going to function reliably year after year.

Step 5: Adopt Brand Management Best Practices

Establishing and employing Brand Best Practices doesn't have be an arduous task but it does take careful thought. One of the best ways to get started is to have a look at what truly successful brands are doing and don't limit your research to just your market niche. Some of the most innovative ideas have come as a result of recognizing best practices in one industry and then adapting them to work in a completely different business sector.

Here are the top four best practices that are, in my opinion, consistent with the most successful brands.

1. Be Customer Focused
2. Be Unique
3. Be Values-Driven, Have a Mission and Vision
4. Be Proactive – Make Offers

Be Customer Focused

Any successful business owner will tell you that developing a strong brand has more to do with earning a good reputation than it does with achieving wide recognition of your logo. This is why staying focused on serving your customers, solving their problems and exceeding their expectations is such as important practice. This kind of customer obsession is the secret sauce behind every successful brand.

Amazon.com is recognized as one of the most customer-focused companies on the planet. As an example, when Amazon CEO, Jeff Bezos, holds a meeting he leaves one seat empty at the conference room table and says that seat is occupied by the "the most important person in the room – the customer".

Apple is another great brand renowned for its customer service. One of its policies requires that all upper management must read customer emails on regular basis. CEO **Tim Cook** sets the trend by reading customer emails every day.

Be Unique

Standing out from the crowd involves more than establishing a unique brand name and logo. Your business must have a Unique Selling Proposition (USP), key messages and personality as compared to your competition. Having a USP is what will set your brand apart and draw new clients closer.

When it comes to the key messages that form the foundation of your UPS, it's been well established that platitudes like "Quality Service" and "Knowledgeable Staff" don't work anymore.

So, rather than using the same tired old phrases you hear everywhere, take a little time to define your unique selling proposition or, USP, based on what's important to your customers.

As an example,

"Acme Auto Accessories offers the only iridescent headlight fluid refill that enhances your night vision. It comes with a lifetime guarantee so you'll never have to worry or stress over driving in the dark again."

Needless to say there's no such thing as headlight fluid but this sample USP does several important things.

1. It positions the product as unique.
2. It identifies a customer problem and solves it: the worry and stress of night driving.
3. It identifies a key benefit: enhanced night vision and,
4. It eliminates purchase risk with a guarantee.

Before you attempt to craft your own USP remember is must be based on:

1. a specific customer profile (The Who) and
2. a specific customer problem (The Why) and,
3. it should contain a unique offer (The What).

Dominos Pizza had one of the best USPs ever,

> *"You get fresh, hot pizza delivered to your door in 30 minutes or less—or it's free."*

Again, it solved a problem and offered a guarantee. What's interesting about this USP is that quality isn't part of the promise. Fresh, hot and on time is what they promise because Dominos knew that's what their best customers (students) wanted.

In addition to a USP every great business has a unique story and personality that its customers can identify with. It can be a story of overcoming adversity, or achieving personal success.

As an example, Roxanne Quimby starting making candles from the unused wax of Burt Shavitz's bee hives. They hit it off and to this day Burt's Bees has remained true to a very simple ideal they both share:

"What you put on your body should be made from the best nature has to offer."

Burt's Bees is now one of the top 50 internationally trusted brands.

Toms Shoes unique story goes like this;
Founder Blake Mycoskie witnessed the hardships faced by children growing up without shoes while traveling in Argentina. He wanted to help so he created Toms Shoes:

"A company that would match every pair of shoes purchased with a new pair of shoes for a child in need."

Be Values-Driven, Have a Clear Mission and Vision

Your brand should stand for something, so take the time to clearly identify your business values, mission and vision. It might be something global like valuing environmental sustainability or something more immediate like supporting your local community. Whatever it is, be true to your values and what you believe in. This practice will lead to building a brand based on loyal, like-minded customers.

Not every company believes in having a values based mission statement but those who do certainly seem to be among the most successful.

The Whole Foods mission statement looks like this:

With great courage, integrity and love—we embrace our responsibility to co-create a world where each of us, our communities, and our planet can flourish. All the while, celebrating the sheer love and joy of food.

Patagonia's Mission statement is;

Build the best product, cause no unnecessary harm, use business to inspire and implement solutions to the environmental crisis.

What Patagonia say about their mission statement is "*a love of wild and beautiful places demands participation in the fight to save them*" and they put their money where their mouth is. Patagonia donates at least 1% of their sales to numerous environmental groups around the world as well as time and services.

Be Proactive and Interactive

Producing a great product or offering a fabulous service is not enough to guarantee success anymore. Unless you implement a marketing system designed to help you easily and effectively prompt your brand on a regular basis it's unlikely your brand will ever be recognized or develop the positive reputation it deserves.

A well-designed marketing system makes use of both traditional and digital media. Traditional marketing can still be effective when used correctly but you can no longer rely solely on this type of 'monologue marketing' as the only method to communication with your audience.

Thanks to social media platforms like Facebook and Twitter, as well as email, your customers share information and experiences about your brand on a regular basis with their family, friends and co-workers. These platforms are the new word of mouth media. What's important to understand about new word of mouth media is that it's impossible to have any real control over what's said about your business, but it is possible to participate in the ongoing conversation.

This is why establishing a strong social media presence and posting regularly accomplishes two things. It's a great way to be proactive about your brand message and it also allows your audience to interact with you and your business.

Step 6: Achieve Online Independence with Content Management Software

As you can probably tell by now I'm big fan of WordPress but I'm not alone. It's the world's most popular Content Management System and for good reason. It's easy to use, it's Open Source and it's been around long enough that it's extremely stable and well supported by developers around the world.

There are other CMS software packages to choose from such as Drupal or Joomla but (in my opinion) they are just not as easy to use as WordPress.

WordPress is Open Source which means, unlike other kinds of software, it's free. The WordPress community works together to ensure that anyone who wants to create a website can do so without having to purchase expensive website development software.

Almost everything you need to know about WordPress can be found at <u>WordPress.org</u> and, of course, on YouTube. There are countless videos on the subject that explain every aspect of how the software works.

You can also visit my website **PowerBrandBuilder.com** where you'll find a complete library of training videos. There is no cost or obligation to access the WordPress training videos we have posted there. Simply create an account and the entire training library is at your fingertips.

There is a lot more that can be said in support of WordPress but I think the best testimonial for this website development tool is that virtually all of the top names in Information Marketing use it.

Step 7:
Avoid Tyranny, Demand Transparency and Training

Transparency is a critical attribute that you need to look for in anyone you choose to do business with. If your web designer or webmaster isn't prepared to let you "look under the hood" or offer you training, walk away.

Websites can be complicated, just like a car, with lots of sophisticated systems all coming together to make a smooth running, easy-to-use device that will get you where you want to go.

But just like a car, you don't have to know everything there is to know about your website to get in the driver's seat and use it to reach your prospective customers and clients. This is especially true if you choose to use WordPress or other content management based software.

It's easier now than it's ever been to change text, upload images or even post a blog.

It's been my experience that the more my clients know about their website, the more successful they are in getting their brand recognized online, and in growing their business.

If your website has been properly structured and is on an automated backup plan there's absolutely no reason why you can't have complete access to your site and make changes to it whenever you want. After all it's the center of your brand online.

Good training is the key to brand independence online. Your web developer or webmaster has an obligation to show you how your website has been structured, how you can change its content, and how any special features you asked for actually work.

So before you commission anyone to build or redesign your website ask what kind of training they offer. One-to-one is still the best in my estimation but be certain that it's not just a demonstration. You need to be in the driver's seat, so that you're the one pushing the buttons, navigating the dashboard and making mistakes. It's how we all learn.

Manuals and videos are great training tools but they shouldn't be the only ways your developer helps you to learn how your website works.

WordPress.org as well as YouTube offer lots of great training absolutely free and if you're not afraid to dive in by yourself you'll find there's no end to the tutorials available. lynda.com is also a great training resource but they do charge for enrolment.

With every new WordPress website I create, I offer two hours of one-to-one training for my clients along with access to a library of videos on how their website works.

If you're interested in learning how to use WordPress to get your message out there and amplify for brand, just visit my free training website **PowerBrandBuilder.com**.

Membership is free and inside you get access to a series of easy-to-follow videos that will show you everything you need to know to take control of your WordPress website.

There are 31 videos in total and the series covers everything from how to install WordPress, straight through to customizing the design of your website.

Step 8: Registering Your Business Name, Brand Name, Trade Name and Trademark

First of all, please understand I am not a lawyer and I am not offering legal advice. This is a big topic that goes beyond the scope of this book but here's an overview.

There are big differences between a trademark, a domain name, your official business name and a trade name. As a business owner it's very important that you understand these differences.

Remember, registering your official business name with your local Joint Stock Registry is an absolute necessity, even if you're just a one man band. Registering nationally is necessary if you plan to set up offices or a franchise outside your local jurisdiction.

In short, if you don't register an official business name and get it approved by your state or provincial authorities you can find yourself in big trouble with the taxman as well as your local government.

A trade name, on the other hand, is like an official nickname for your business. As an example, when I started out on my own as a video producer, I registered a limited company called Duncan Moss Productions Ltd.
As my company grew, and I hired staff and started offering web design and marketing services, I decided that my official company name didn't adequately represent all my business had to offer and so I registered the official trade name, Moss Media Solutions.

As far as the taxman and the bank are concerned Moss Media Solutions is just another name for the Duncan Moss Productions Ltd. but our clients and suppliers know us better as Moss Media Solutions.

A trademark is something very special and is a very different thing than a business name, a trade name or a domain name.
Registering a trademark takes time and money and should be given serious consideration if you want protection for your brand on a national level. A trademark protects brand names and logos used on goods and services.

For example, if you invent a new kind of mousetrap, you would apply for a patent to protect your invention. But you would also apply to register a trademark to protect the brand name of your new mouse trap.

> **Tip 7**
> *As an aside, you might also copyright the TV commercial you use to advertise your trademarked mouse trap. Copyright is another tool you can use to protect things like scripts, books, eBooks and website text.*

So you see, domain names, business names, trade names, trademarks, patents and copyright are all different tools you can use to protect different parts of your business.

Your trademark name may be the same as your domain name but they are two very different things.

Just because you've registered your business or brand name as a .com or .ca domain, doesn't mean that other people can't use it. It only means they can't create a .com or .ca website using that name.

A trademark unlike a domain name or business name identifies goods or services as being from a particular source.

It's important to understand that under the law, just because you have purchased a domain name from a domain name registrar does not give you any trademark rights.

For example, even if you register a particular domain name, say BobsAutobody.com, later on you could be required to give it up if it infringes on someone else's trademark rights.

The same can true for a business name. As a rule, whoever is first in registering a particular name as a trademark generally wins any dispute over ownership of the same business name or domain name. So even if you're the first person to register a particular domain name and business name, but don't bother to register it as a trademark, you could lose the use of that name to someone else who gets it trademarked later on.

Once you decide that the type of brand protection you need is trademark protection then selecting a mark or logo is the first step in the application and registration process.

This must be done with care, because not every logo can register as a trademark to be legally protectable.

It's not unusual for business owners who are new to trademarks to choose a mark for their product or service that is difficult or impossible to register.

The reasons are too varied to go into here, but because there is much more to registering a trademark than meets the eye, you will most likely need the help of a trademark lawyer or a trademark service.

Before filing for a trademark, you will probably need help figuring out whether it is can actually be registered and how difficult it will be to protect it. That's because protecting it will be up to you. The government only registers it. The same is true by the way for your domain name.

There are 3 basic types of trademarks: a standard character mark, a stylized/design mark, or a sound mark.

Because a trademark must be associated with a specific product or service, it's imperative that you clearly identify the exact product or service your trademark will apply to.

It all starts by searching the United States Patent and Trademark Office or Industry Canada database to find out whether someone else has already claimed similar trademark rights.

Before filing an application, you must know your basis for filing. In other words, you must be able to justify the need for your trademark and explain how it will be used in connection with your product or service.

Getting all this done is easier now than it used to be because you can file for a trademark online. Here are a few links you should find useful.

http://www.trademarkcanada.org

https://www.ic.gc.ca/eic/site/cipointernet-internetopic.nsf/eng/wr01369.html

http://www.uspto.gov/

The fees required to file are non-refundable processing fees, and just because you paid the fees doesn't guarantee your trademark application will be approved.

The other thing to know about all of this is that it's not fast. It can take months before your application is processed.

This review includes a search for conflicting trademarks, and a thorough examination of your written application, drawings and specifications.

If your trademark application is rejected for minor reasons, there is a chance you can reapply after making the needed adjustments but you will have to pay the application fees again and wait again.

If your trademark receives preliminary approval and is made public, you'll have to wait to see if anyone objects to your claim.

If no one opposes your trademark claim, you will then be given permission to use it, but even then, it is not a fully certified and registered trademark.

How you use it will determine if you will be allowed to finally get it certified and fully registered. And so, you will be required to provide additional documentation after preliminary approval has been received.

This whole process can vary quite a bit based on whether you are applying for a US or Canadian trademark, but the basic principles remain the same.

You must assume responsibility for the protection and defense of your trademark just as you would your overall brand.

Now that we've managed to slog our way through all the technical stuff, it's time to take a really good look at how you actually develop a brand and manage its reputation.

Step 9: Build and Grow Your Brand Platform

One of the most important strategies you can employ to protect your brand is reputation management. But before we dive straight into this prickly topic let's review what the heck a brand really is.

So often the word brand is associated with a logo, a trademark, or how you present your business to the public.

If you've gone to the trouble of carefully choosing a name for your business, registering it in all the right places, launching a website, getting signage, printing business cards and doing all those things every business owner does to establish a unique presence for their business, you might think you have a brand. But as I mentioned at the outset, even after all that work, most small businesses don't actually have a brand.

By contrast, here are a few companies you're sure to recognize that have achieved true brand status:

- Apple
- GoodYear
- Nike
- Coca-Cola and
- Google

It's true, these are all large international brands, but if a perfect stranger were asked to name ten of the top businesses in your city or niche, would your business come to mind? You might be one of the few lucky business owners who can say yes with certainty, but for most of us we know that our business hasn't achieved a top ten brand status even in our own home town.

One of the key reasons for this is that nearly everyone is exposed to more than 3,000 competing advertising messages every day, making it extremely difficult for the average business to cut through and get noticed. Worse still, people have learned to ignore advertising or have become blind to ads that are in our field of vision. This 'ad blindness' makes getting noticed and achieving a brand status even more difficult.

As a business owner, you probably know that cutting through the advertising clutter and noise to establish brand recognition is a very expensive and time consuming process. You can only imagine how much time and money Apple or Coca-Cola have invested so that the minute you hear their name or see their logo you know exactly what they offer and how you feel about their product or service.

If you take a look at well-known brands in your area like the biggest car dealership or most popular radio station, again you can be certain that a great deal of money, time and strategic marketing has gone into establishing those business names as brands.

Business that have actually achieved brand status can afford to indulge in brand based advertising. What this means is that they don't have to concern themselves with making a specific offer, or telling their audience why their product or service is better, every time they advertise. Businesses with real brand status can simply flash their logo or attach it to a feel-good message and in doing so maintain their market share.

You see, a real brand is what's referred to as top-of-mind. In other words, it occupies a very special place in your short-term memory that thousands of other business are competing for every single day. If your business isn't top-of-mind in your niche, even on a local basis, then unfortunately you don't have a brand.

This is why brand based marketing is such a waste of money for most businesses. So what's the solution? Why bother to try and protect something you don't really have?

The real alternative to brand based marketing is direct response marketing. A simple search on Google will offer up a tremendous amount of information on the topic, if you'd like to know more.

In short, it's marketing that focuses on your clients' problems and offers a solution based on a unique selling proposition. This is the polar opposite of traditional shotgun style advertising that tries to get people to remember the name of your business by bombarding them repeatedly with the same message.

The direct response approach to marketing leads prospective clients to consider your solution to their problem which can then lead to sales. It's a far more effective way to reach people who need what you have to offer than fighting for brand recognition with hundreds, possibly thousands, of other businesses who have more to spend on advertising than you do. As for protecting your brand, let's go back to that early Wikipedia definition of brand:

> A brand is a name or symbol that distinguishes one seller's product from its competitors. A brand is also the personality or reputation of a business based on how its customers and staff perceive it.

The reputation side of your brand is far more important to the success of your business than the instant recognition of your logo or business name will ever be.

So, even though you may not have a well-recognized brand in the bigger sense of the word, you now know what steps you must take to protect your brand name and symbol.

The good news is that when it comes to reputation there is a lot you can do to manage and protect it. The secret is not to focus all your efforts on old school logo based marketing. Instead, you're much better off growing and managing your business by developing and leveraging a brand platform.

This is a very old concept that's been remodeled for the digital age. In short, it's what you use to stand out and be heard in a crowded market place.

More specifically, a business platform is a carefully constructed communication system, best suited to your style, that supports the growth of an ongoing conversation with more of your best customers.

Another way to describe this is the proactive use of a complementary set of media tools you use to encourage your prospects and clients to learn and talk about the unique nature of your products and services.

To grow a solid platform, you must offer real value as well as an opportunity for honest feedback that allows your audience to respond to the personality of your business.

Unlike in the old days of monologue marketing, the construction of a brand platform is based more on a dialogue with subscribers, contacts and followers rather than snappy slogans, catchy jingles and gimmick advertising. Without a strong and loyal following, there is no conversation, no reputation to speak of, and no sales.

A well-tuned business platform revives the lost art of conversation to ensure that your target audience is not just hearing about your business through word of mouth or anonymous posts by internet trolls.

It is by far the best way to establish a well-recognized brand because it builds a positive reputation based on two-way communication.

So let's look more closely at what you can do to establish a positive reputation for your business by managing and growing your brand platform.

I can't stress the importance of this enough because if you don't take action to leverage the power of a brand platform, very few people will ever know the name of your business let alone its reputation. As a result of not knowing your business (or you), prospective customers can't possibly like or trust what you have to offer enough to commit to a purchase.

The good news is that your platform can be constructed using the kind of media and communications vehicles you're most comfortable with. But it should include at least three different ways to communicate if it's going to be truly successful.

If you're comfortable with things like Facebook and email, be sure to make them a part of your platform. But since both of these communication tools are digital you should consider adding some form of print media into the mix, like direct mail or a newsletter. And don't forget about one-to-one communication as well as public speaking. They're still two of the best ways to reach your audience.

It should go without saying that your website needs to be part of your platform and to really get the most out of your website, you should consider a blog.

If you're just starting out, your platform and your message should not be brand focused. Instead it should be client focused, explaining the problems you solve for them and the unique nature of the solution you offer.

Having decided on the media you're most comfortable with, it's time to put a system in place for content creation and distribution.

A blog is often a great place to start. Finding time to write a blog can be a challenge, but if you commit to posting something short once a week or even once a month you'll find it easier to do as time goes on.

If you plan in advance, you can create a series of posts on a particular topic that, later on, can be combined to create an eBook on your area of expertise.

When you've posted something to your blog, you can then promote it on Facebook, Google+ and Twitter. You can even add your blog link to the bottom of your emails, inviting everyone you email to read your latest post.

Blog posts can also be used as the basis of PowerPoint presentations that can then be turned into live presentations or even videos.

As you can see, the idea is to leverage your work by re-purposing it for use in a variety of media. At first glance this strategy may seem redundant but since not everyone reads blogs, or likes Facebook it's important to distribute your content as widely as possible.

The object in developing a platform is to establish an audience and your authority in your business niche. Even modest progress in this regard will go a long way in establishing a positive reputation for you as someone who is willing to help others and share their knowledge.

Unfortunately, choosing to say nothing about your business and rely on word of mouth marketing is not a good choice in this age of social media dominance. That's because if you say nothing, others will fill the void but it may not always be what you'd like said about your business.

The real secret to developing a solid platform for your business is to put a system in place that ensures you will distribute new content on a consistent basis. On again off again won't build an audience and in turn won't help you build a positive reputation.

If you'd like to know more about developing your platform, best-selling author Michael Hyatt has an excellent book on the subject, entitled "Platform: Get Noticed in a Noisy World". Here's a link to his book.

https://michaelhyatt.com/products/platform-hardcover-book

Take-aways and Closing Thoughts

To Brand or Not to Brand
>A brand is more than just a logo. It's your reputation and it must be carefully nurtured in order to enjoy real success. That's why 'brand advertising' is a waste of time.

Website Orphans and Hijackings are Preventable
>The time and effort required to protect your brand far outweigh the potentially devastating consequences of doing nothing.

The Wild West of Website Development
>Because website development is unregulated as compared to other equally important business services, business owners must take it upon themselves to put safeguards in place that will protect their business name, website and brand.

The Keys to the Kingdom
>Whoever controls the passwords to your website and hosting package holds the keys to your online kingdom. Don't hand them over to strangers.

Don't Commit to What You Don't Understand
>Basic online brand management is easy to understand so don't be fooled by the baffle-gab out there. Reputable service providers offer easy-to-understand terms of service, in writing, along with one-to-one training and support.

You Have every Right to Be In the Driver's Seat
>Managing your brand online is a lot like driving a car. You don't have to know how to build one to control one.

Demand Transparency
>Online marketing and website development are not rocket science anymore. If your developer or marketing firm can't clearly explain their deliverables to you, walk away.

Build a Platform
>Connecting with prospective clients and staying in touch with customers is all about the art of conversation. Monologue marketing is dead.

Additional Resources

Download my free buyer's guide *"How to Hire a Web Designer"*. It's sure to save you a great deal of grief and money.

You might also like my *"Why WordPress"* report and my **White Paper on Internet Marketing**. They are all free for the taking and available on my website **BrandPowerBuilder.com**

If you'd like to know more about using WordPress for your website I offer a free step-by step WordPress video training series. It's available to anyone who subscribes to my website.

Lastly, one to one coaching is also available so feel free to contact me for a no obligation consultation.

info@BrandPowerBuilder.com

902-404-9854

Brand Power Builder System

If you're interested in seeing exactly how the **Brand Power Builder System** works and what's inside the tool kit just visit **BrandPowerBuilder.com** to watch the training video.

www.ingramcontent.com/pod-product-compliance
Lightning Source LLC
Chambersburg PA
CBHW070107210526
45170CB00013B/775